SMARTER, FASTER, WEALTHIER
EVERYDAY FINANCIAL TOPICS

RODERICK JEFFERSON

CONTENTS

About the Author   v
Foreword   xi

1. Basic wealth building   1
2. Change equals growth   5
3. Budgeting   9
4. Understanding Credit   15
5. Credit Score   17
6. Debt - Why do you hate it   21
7. Understanding Interest Rates   25
8. Risk vs Reward   35
9. Investing   39
10. Stocks   43
11. Bonds   47
12. Life Insurance   49
13. Term Life Insurance   53
14. Whole Life Insurance   55
15. Retirement Planning   59
16. Types of Retirement plans   63
17. Build A Team   67

ABOUT THE AUTHOR

My story is similar to that of many others. I grew up in Florida, in a working-class household. I had the pleasure of having both my parents around. My parents were always open and honest about money. There were times when money was tight, and there were times when money was flowing, and we would even take vacations to water parks. By working hard, I was lucky enough to get a college football scholarship that helped pay for some of my education. Football took me many places and taught me so much discipline. I was never the biggest guy on the team, but I learned hard work from my parents, and I carried that with me into every practice and every game. I left college with a business management degree and continued to play football in the Indoor Football League. I played for 5 years before I decided to call it quits and focus on starting a new career. At that point, I had come to terms with the fact that my dream of the NFL was over, and that I needed to focus on a career path. This is what led me deeper down the path of finance. I have been in finance since 2004, working for Merrill lynch during my off seasons. But in 2007, I was approached by a senior management team member about becoming a financial advisor. Now, I had no idea what that was really like since no one I knew was a financial advisor. I job shadowed with a younger advisor for an entire day and fell in love with the idea of helping people while being able to spend time with my family. From that day on, I pursued the idea of becoming a financial advisor. I finally got that chance when I was hired by Fidelity in 2010 as a financial advisor. I passed all my tests and began training. My eyes were opened to the vast world of not only investing, but wealth building. I learned that this information is not exclusive; it just wasn't taught in households like mine. I gained more and more knowledge as the years went by and I began helping others. I felt I could be the bridge that could carry this information into my culture, but I just didn't know how. I assumed it would happen naturally since I was an African American who wanted to help his fellow African Americans learn about these wealth-building techniques, but I didn't understand at that time how hard it was to overcome years of cultural conditioning. Now here we are; 10 years later and I'm writing a book. I never thought I could write a book, but my passion for helping as many people as possible helped flood the words onto the pages. In this year of 2020, aka the "year of Covid" and "year of Black lives matter", I couldn't sit by and do nothing. I had to help people in some way. This most recent financial crisis and the continued systemic racism has made financial literacy even more important. Many studies have shown Blacks and Hispanics, when given the opportunity typically don't invest and in turn, earn less return on their money. Research also shows this is because in minority culture, financial literacy is much lower than in that of our White counterparts. In my effort to increase financial literacy in minority culture, I wrote this book. I hope you not only learn and enjoy it, but take action and grow your wealth. To obtain knowledge is only one part of the equation; you must work on the whole problem if you want to see true results.

As stated on Investopedia, "Financial literacy is the ability to understand and effectively apply various financial skills, including personal financial management, budgeting, and investing." Financial literacy helps individuals become self-sufficient so that they can achieve financial stability. Now, why is this important for you to know? According to a study by FINRA Foundation NFCS in 2018, despite the economy recovering dramatically, the gap between people who struggled financially and those who were financially successful was still wide. The largest gaps coming from young people, low-income earners, and African Americans, while White survey takers have remained steady in saving since the recovery in 2009. The African American community has decreased by 6%. This means that over the 9 years; from 2009 to 2018, African Americans have not been able to save as much as their White counterparts. Only three in ten Americans with an income under 25k are able to save. This number is even lower than it was in 2009, according to FINRA Foundation NFCS. The link between those who have financial education and those who do not has shown up in everyday financial behavior. Of the people surveyed, the ones with some financial education had better financial habits and behaviors such as not overdrawing their account, limiting credit card debt, and taking less bank loans; meaning they pay cash. Statistically, we as African Americans are more likely to overdraw our checking accounts than any other ethnicity. African Americans are 34% more likely to overdraw their account than White Americans. Hispanics are 22% more likely to overdraw their account than White Americans, as per the 2018 survey. Now, this can be attributed to the higher percentage of African Americans being low-income earners; a systematic racism that has denied us the necessary capital to build wealth and start businesses like the other ethnicities. I think there is another part of the equation; the lack of financial education in the country and especially in the Black community. Facts are; it's hard to have a thriving financial education system in the Black community when we are still facing hurdles in our struggle for equality. This is one of the compelling reasons I decided to write this book. We need to increase our financial literacy so we can begin to not only build wealth, but create legacies and generational wealth. This can only be done if we are able to further understand money from a perspective outside of spending. I encourage everyone to ask themselves this question, "Are you subtracting or are you multiplying?" The financial decisions you make today will help shape your financial future. If you are going down to borrow money from a payday loan to pay your credit card bill, then these are behaviors I'm directly speaking to. The interest rate on the credit card is already high, most likely 29%, plus the interest on the money you took in advance—this just perpetuates a cycle that sometimes we can never get out of. 50% of African Americans use non-bank borrowing methods such as income tax advances and payday loans. Now comparing that to other ethnicities, Hispanics, with 38% are the closest and Whites are the lowest, with 23%. If we can make overall better financial decisions, we can keep from digging ourselves a deeper grave. We are going to discuss how to develop better habits, as well as increase your financial education around topics that affect the decisions you make every day.

FOREWORD

Only 57% of all of America is financially literate according to the Milken Institute. I first found this number to be very shocking, considering we are the wealthiest country in the world. This made me dig a little deeper and I discovered that the African American community, which is the culture I belong to, has an even lower number when it comes to financial literacy. I believe the low financial literacy for African American households is part of the reason we control only 3% of the nation's wealth according to Brookings.edu. To uncover the other reason why African Americans control only 3% of the nation's wealth according to Brookings.edu, we have to go back a little bit in history so bear with me. I like to say that this all started with the 40 acres and a mule. You might be thinking, what happened to the "40 acres and a mule" and why is it even important? It was meant to help the transition from slavery into freedom. General William Sherman claimed hundreds of thousands of acres of land once owned by Whites and split into 40-acre plots so it could be used for Black settlements. Congress also established the Freedman's savings bank to give Blacks the ability to gain financial freedom. Though these things would not have made up for the 400 years of slavery, it would have given Blacks a place to start with ownership and banks with fair lending practices. What started as a good plan was shot down once Lincoln was assassinated in the theater on the night of April 15, 1865. Once Andrew Johnson took over as president, he rescinded the Sherman claim of land from White plantation owners. The land, at this time had over 400,000 Blacks—who would later be pushed out—settled on it. The Freedmen's bank, which was run by a board of White trustees, also folded; it had over one million in Black deposits. Now, who made a series of bad loans which ultimately bankrupted the Freedman's bank?

I'm only bringing these topics up to point out the fact that Blacks not only suffered through slavery, but also suffered the disappointment of a failed promise; by which we are still feeling the effects as they echo through generations. African Americans also suffered through Redlining and bias systems that were put in place to cripple their pursuit of wealth. Our lack of voting rights, which were not fully restored until 1965 also prevented us from participating in the process to help change the systematic racism that still exists today. Now that we have a basic idea of how the wealth gap was perpetuated, let's begin to look at how we can close the gap. Having Black billionaires or even a Black president is not enough, though those are milestone accomplishments. We have to address the fact that the Black culture as a whole needs to close the gap. One of the ways through which we can do this is by increasing our financial literacy. This is because we make financial decisions daily; whether it's accepting a job offer, figuring out the kind of house you can afford to purchase, deciding if you should borrow money to buy that car, or swiping your credit card. These are all financial decisions that can shape your future. For example; a bad loan today could turn into years of debt, but if you understand your finances better and you know how finances work, you can make smarter decisions and even learn to make your money work for you.

CHAPTER 1
BASIC WEALTH BUILDING

We hear the term "stacks and racks" most often used in song lyrics or even in conversation in among people in our community, though the word we really need to learn is 'wealth'. So for those of you who don't know what 'stacks' are, pay attention. A Stack equals ten racks, and one rack equals $1000, which means a stack is $10,000. This concludes your lesson in hip hop economics. Just like the word stacks, wealth is a form of measurement. Wealth is defined as a measure of value of all assets of worth owned by a person. Another way to look at it is; wealth is the measure or the accumulation of a scarce resource, which in most cases, money is that resource. Thinking back to my high school and college years, I had the perspective on money that I learned from my culture, as well as the perspective on money I learned from other cultures. Though I think the greatest impact was from my parents. They kept an open an honest communication with me when it came to money. They helped me understand that the clothes I liked or the shoes I wanted were not free, and that the money used to pay for those things came from their hard work. I once heard someone say that your mind will always rob you of the opportunity money gave you, therefore, you must break the culture of it. You gain something by being in a household that talks about money and prosperity. It helps you develop a better process for finding solutions when it comes to money. This is a book For The Culture. I'm an African American, and throughout the years, I have heard many different perspectives on money; most of which were from other African Americans who I was either related to or were friends with. At the time I was hearing these information, I thought it was good advice; though truly, some were. Once I hit college, not only did I start developing my own perspective on money, I began to learn about other people outside my culture's perspectives on money. The first thing I would notice when I speak to people outside my culture was the difference between our stories around money. Like my parents would always say, "You can't keep up with the Jones". This was usually said after I asked for something expensive because one of the kids at school had it. I was always told to focus on my schoolwork so that I can get a good job one day—as if a good job was the solution to financial problems. Now, let me say this about my parents; they were AWESOME! They were the kind of parents that believed in hard work and always doing your best. They both worked blue collar jobs and raised two wonderful kids; and even helped raise a few nieces and nephews in the process. To say my parents knew how to make a dollar out of 15 cents was an understatement. Now that I have hopefully saved myself from my first spanking in 30 years, back to my point. When my friends from outside my culture spoke about money, they talked about it differently, almost as if money was a tool and not a solution. Of course, this didn't make sense to me at first because I was taught from the perspective that money was a solution. Having more of it meant no bills, more clothes in the closet, bigger house, and being able to help those around me. I had never thought of money as a tool; like a hammer that could be used to build or create something. In my culture, many of us dream of making enough money to buy our parents a house or use it to get into a better neighborhood; and all these things are solutions to a situation. As I progressed through school and got my first job in Finance at a prominent investment firm, I became surrounded by more and more people who thought of money as a tool rather than a solution. Here I was, talking to people who used money to make more money by investing and using it to build business and creating jobs— and they were successful doing it. Being surrounded by all this success and wisdom made me start to see money from a different point of view. I want you to understand that money is a tool and not a solution. I want you to come away from this book with the mindset of wanting to build wealth, and trust me, you can. The very fact that you're reading this book already gives you a greater head start, unlike I, or your parents. In order to build wealth, the first thing you have to do is open your mind to change and new ideas, which for most of you, this will be your first-time hearing about how to build wealth. The second thing you will have to do is take action. Take the steps and skills learned in this book and apply them to your daily life. No, you won't build wealth overnight. But you will find that one good decision leads to another and before long, you will look back and see how far you've come, compared to when your parents were at your age.

Employment will destroy your gift. Our culture has conditioned us to go get an education so we can get a stable job. Rarely do we have discussions about creating things; like a business. I'm not saying working a job is bad—I'm working a job right now. What I'm saying is that our culture has to shift and start having conversations about using money as a tool we have in learning this process, and pass on the knowledge of investing, starting our own business, buying real estate, to name a few. We have to learn how we can take one dollar and turn it into two dollars. We must not be afraid to take certain risk; in order to reap the rewards, we have to take a calculated risk. Make sure you are open to new things—if you want something different you must do something different. In this book, I will teach you some easy financial concepts around money that will allow you to make better financial decisions and remove some of the fear that stands in your way of building wealth.

CHAPTER 2
CHANGE EQUALS GROWTH

First, I want to say my sister is averse to change. She is a great example of this. She went to the doctor one day and they advised her to increase her activity level because her health numbers were increasing in areas that could be dangerous down the road. So, me being the workout warrior that I am, decided it's time she started working out. I sent her some home workout gears and all kinds of workout information. Whenever I called her and ask if she worked out, she always said no, or had an excuse as to why she couldn't that day. One thing about real true change is that, you can't make someone's mind want it. I love my sister to death, but that was not enough to make her change her habit. Once her mind about her health changed and she accepted the fact she couldn't do this alone, she hired a trainer; though she complained at first and she dreaded each workout—it was 3 times a week. I can say I'm proud of her because despite her hatred for workout, she pushed through. As she started seeing results, I could see her mindset change; she didn't want her results to stop. My sister began to crave for the results; she didn't like working out, but she liked the results. She even planned how to handle the holiday eating and traveling with her trainer because, her mind was now associated with working out and getting positive results. My sister reached her goal and till date, continues to work out with her trainer. Nothing like the power of a changed mind. Once you accept the change and make the goal personal, there is truly nothing you can't overcome.

Making better financial decisions requires change —and change is hard. Whenever you make changes in life, it means you have to give something up, which is not easy. Especially, because our brains are hard wired to help us avoid pain, some have considered the emotional pain of change to be the same as losing a loved one. So when you start the process of changing your spending habits, it is best to start in small steps. First, focus on the reason you're making the change; and just being debt free is not enough. Write down what being debt free will do for you; make it personal. Maybe it allows you to buy a home, provide for your family or whatever it is that is near and dear to you. Second, write out a strategy of how you plan to take action on the changes you need to make. This helps because you will face tough times that will drag you back to your old habits. However, if you have a written plan, you are more likely to stick with it despite the hurdles you may have to jump. Third, track your progress. I mean really track it, not just a mental check mark. Look at your budget weekly and see if it matches your actual spending. This has been proven to help attain real results and create a new habit, which is what we want. The fourth step is look at your goal and remind yourself why you're doing this and what this change will empower you to do. This is great for you emotionally as you see yourself getting closer to the goal. This will give you the energy you need to push forward because I guarantee you that every day, your mind will be trying to convince you to just stop this foolishness and go back to your old ways. But you need to remain strong. This fourth step will also help with a recharge. These four steps will help you not only develop a strategy but help you stay on track and reach your goal.

CHAPTER 3
BUDGETING

'Budgeting'. What is that? Most people say they have a budget but let's keep it real. Only 25% of Americans have a written budget according to a Schwab 2019 Modern Wealth Index study. Most of us use some form of a mental budget or balled up receipts in our pocket; which is proven to be ineffective. For African Americans, only 1 in 5 have six months of emergency savings set aside. 33% of African Americans have less than one month of funds set aside. When surveyed, most African Americans said their biggest regret was, not saving or investing early enough. One of the reasons I started writing this book is to increase the financial literacy in America, but especially in the African American community. I think that budgeting or being able to create a proper budget is one of the most important tools you can use to create wealth. When we talk of budgeting, most of us think of this as restrictive or limiting; which doesn't sound fun. So I ask that you think of budgeting like a luxury car, an s550 Mercedes Benz for example. Think of your income as gas and Mercedes only take premium. Now the first thing you have to do is put gas in the car, which is your income. Because a Mercedes does not run on your hopes and dreams, if you don't put gas in it, you won't go anywhere. Each one of your goals and your expenses are a destination. In order to reach your destination, you have to have gas; which in this example, is your income.

You must break down your income into monthly amounts and subtract your expenses and goals (i.e., emergency savings), and this, is called budgeting. For instance; let's say one of your goals is to go to Jamaica. If you want to go to Jamaica, you would calculate the cost it would take to fly, rent a hotel, eat and have fun while you're there. So a proper budget for this vacation would be something like this. 1. Flight cost, 2. Hotel cost, 3. Daily eating expense, and 4.fun money. You would total all those costs together and then divide it by the time frame of which you plan to take this trip, let's say 5 months from now. By doing this, you will know exactly how much you need to save every month in order to make this vacation possible. Budgeting is something that everyone can do, but it does take discipline. Also, studies have shown that if you write things down you're more likely to accomplish them.

So what does a proper budget look like? A budget should be detailed and be set for a specific time frame—I prefer monthly. In a detailed budget, you're going to include everything from your expenses, your savings goals, your vacation goals, your retirement goals, your debt payoff plan, and any other goals you look to accomplish in the short term and also, in the long term. You want to break these goals down into monthly or even in some cases, weekly budget plans; such as how much I'm going to spend on lunch each week. This can really add up. By writing the budget down and reviewing it at minimum on a monthly basis, you will be able to find yourself staying on track and reaching your budgeting goals more often than if you just write down annual budget goals and review them once a year. One of the keys to budgeting is sitting down and thinking about what are the goals you want to accomplish in the short and long term. This will allow you to plan out and have a more detailed budget, and in addition, help prioritize your finances.

The following is a list of steps showing how you can begin to set up a budget and prioritize your finances better.

Step one; think about and write down your goals and list them in order of short and long term. For example; Jamaica vacation in five months would be short term. Payoff credit cards in three years would be long term. After that, prioritize them based on when they need to be completed.

Step two; write out all your necessary expenses like rent, water, etc., and break them down into monthly payments.

Step three; write down your income and subtract all your expenses and your emergency savings fund and see what you have left over. The extra money that is left is what will be used to pay for the vacation or pay off the debt. So you will need to subtract that total amount (vacation or debt) from the money that was left over after expenses.

Monthly Expenses		
ITEM	DUE DATE	AMOUNT
Rent/mortgage	Date	$1,400.00
Electric	Date	$120.00
Gas	Date	$80.00
Cell phone	Date	$70.00
Groceries	Date	$100.00
Car payment	Date	$500.00
Water	Date	$70.00
Credit cards	Date	$80.00
Auto Insurance	Date	$100.00
Gym	Date	$25.00
Cable	Date	$120.00
Miscellaneous	Date	$26.00

Monthly Savings	
DATE	AMOUNT
Date	$100.00

Now take the $1,327 left over and apply it to my debt payoff goal, which is $500 a month on the credit card.

$1,327 extra money-$500 credit card=$827 left over for the month. I can make adjustments to my goals if needed.

Now some you might say I don't have very much left over. This is an opportunity to go back and review your expenses and see if there are areas in which you can reduce your expenses, thus increasing the amount of money you have left over. If you're not able to reduce your expenses, then you now know that you need a side hustle. Before you start a side hustle, try moving out your timeframe on your goals. Maybe that vacation needs to be nine months from now instead of five months, and maybe you have to pay off those credit cards in five years instead of three. Budgeting will allow you to create realistic goals so that you don't set yourself up for failure. Because you want to set goals that can ultimately be accomplished, setting a proper budget will make sure that you're putting the right amount of dollars aside for the appropriate amount of time. The key is to understand your unique financial situation so that you can make informed financial decisions moving forward.

CHAPTER 4
UNDERSTANDING CREDIT

Back in August of 2008, the financial crisis had just started to take hold, and I was moving from St. Louis Mo back to my hometown, Jacksonville, FL. I had job interviews lined up, so in my mind, I was only going to be without a job for a month at most. I was going to be living with a good friend of mine and pay him rent. When boom! The bottom fell out and every interview I had lined up got cancelled due to companies freezing their hiring. So here I was, back in my hometown at 28 years old with no job and grown man bills. As you can imagine, I relied heavily on my credit cards. Just like we all feel when we hit hard times and everything gets thrown at us at once; I had old doctor bills coming in, car note was due, and I owed my buddy rent. I was not very happy to say the least. I got a part time job at a prominent bank which barely covered the rent, meanwhile my credit card limits were getting closer and closer to being maxed out. Thankfully, I survived until I was able to get a full-time job, but I was going to use most of my salary to pay my credit cards every month. I knew I had to do something so I called up the credit card companies and they were willing to work with me. They froze my cards and put me on a repayment plan that I could afford. I can remember the feeling of finally getting those cards paid off. It was a while before I wanted to look at a credit card again. But I know that having good credit is important so I couldn't avoid having another credit card forever. This time, I knew I would handle things differently. This was because after working my new job in banking for so long and spending so much time on the phones working with my credit cards, I had a better understanding of how credit worked and how I could use my credit cards responsibly. In this chapter, we will discuss some of the things I have learned about credit cards and your credit score. With this information, you will be able to make more informed decisions and avoid some of the same mistakes I made.

CHAPTER 5
CREDIT SCORE

The number one thing banks want to know is your FICO SCORE or commonly referred to as credit score. First, you must understand what qualifies as debt. Debt includes credit cards, personal loans from a bank or financial institution, mortgages and car loans, student loans, and unpaid medical bills. And all these affect your credit score. One of the big factors that makes up your score is credit utilization. This makes up 30% of your credit score. Credit utilization is the balance of your card divided by the card limit. Let's break this down further; if you have a card with a $5,000 limit and you use $2,500 of that balance, your credit card utilization is 50%, which is high. As a result, this will drag your credit score down. The ideal goal is to keep your utilization down under 30%; to put that in real numbers, 30% of your $5,000 limit is $1,500. When looking at your credit score, it's also important to look at your on-time payments or payment history; which makes up 35% of your score.

Payment history is simply that, do you pay on time or have you been late more than 30 days? If you are late more than 30 days, you will see missed payment show up in your credit history and it will remain for at least 2 years before it drops off. Before you run out and go cut up your cards you, must first know that length of credit history makes up 15% of your total credit score. So even though you might want to cancel all your cards after reading this, don't. Maintaining those cards are key to your length of credit history, so keep those cards even if you don't use them. Instead, freeze them in a block of ice if you must. New credit accounts lower your average account age which will ultimately lower your overall score. Remember, credit history makes up 15% of your overall score. Opening new credit card accounts only makes up 10% of your overall score. The last piece of your total credit score is the mix of credit. This means, do you use credit cards and loans? Typically, lenders like to see a good mix so they know you have a history of making different types of debt payments, and that you are successful at it. The mix of credit makes up 10% of your overall score. Once you understand your credit score, you will begin to see the ways to borrow responsibly and generate a higher score which will help you get lower rates. TYPICALLY, you want your score between 670 and 740 to be considered for the best rates, but I would advise you to ask the lender what the required score is before you have them run your credit. You want the lowest interest rate possible, therefore the key is to pay the least amount of interest back as allowed by the financing institution.

CHAPTER 6
DEBT - WHY DO YOU HATE IT

Debt. When most people hear that word, the reaction you get is negative. Most hear the term debt and their face turn sour. Many people dream of the day they can say that they have zero debt. This kind of thinking makes sense because in our culture, 84% of African Americans believe financial security is the American dream according to blackenterprise.com. Financial security also means being able to keep every dollar you earn and not owe anybody else. I do believe that having zero debt is a great accomplishment. But on your pursuit to wealth, you will come to understand that there is good debt and bad debt and they are not to be thought of as the same. Think of bad debt as an anchor that drags down your financial goals—high interest rate credit cards are one of the most common types of bad debt. The average interest rate for fair credit borrower is 23.20% according to Wallethub.com. This can make it extremely difficult to pay off even over long periods of time. Imagine you walk into the mall to buy a pair of jeans and the price is $50, but then a salesperson tells you at the register you will have to pay 62.50 plus tax; that's a 25% mark up. Now I know some of us would throw those pants right at the cashier for even speaking such foolishness. But the point is, most of you wouldn't buy those jeans if they had a 25% mark up. That's exactly what we are doing when we make a purchase on a high interest rate credit card. You are paying 25% more than someone who just walks in and pays $50 in cash. Some of you might still be wondering how this hurts you in the long run. When you accumulate a large credit card balance that you can't pay off monthly, it becomes a revolving debt. Which simply means the balance carriers over, month after month until you pay it off completely. But the catch is, each month, any new purchases like those $50 jeans plus any previous balance amount is rolled over an interest is charged. The credit company makes money on the interest we pay them. The interest on credit cards is calculated daily and a credit card company will multiply the current balance by the daily rate. The credit card company is using the power of compounding, which is something we will discuss in another chapter. But those pair of $50 jeans that you do not pay for by the end of the month are now costing you interests every day the balance remains on your credit card. If you kept making the minimum payment on the card, you will be paying mostly interest, which goes to the companies' pocket and your $50 balance will hardly be touched. This kind of revolving debt as it's called, also affects your credit report. This is important because when you walk into a bank and you want to take out a loan for a car, or a mortgage to buy your first home, they will use the credit score to determine your eligibility. As we mentioned earlier when we talked about credit scores, if you have a high score you can get the lowest interest rate. We have spent most of our time discussing bad debt, but as I said, there is good debt to.

A mortgage is an example of good debt. Most of us have to go down to the bank and borrow money to buy a home. I imagine if you're paying cash, you're probably not reading this book. Majority of us get 15- or 30-year mortgages. The reason this is good debt is because your home is an investment, your home can increase in value over time. If you have a very low interest rate, then you're paying down your loan faster. This means when you sell your home, you will most likely get more money than you owe on the home. Here is an example; if I buy a home for 250k with 3% interest and pay on it for 15 years and then I decide to sell since my kids are all grown up now, I will still have to pay off my remaining balance of roughly 151,000. But if I can sell my home for 300k, I can pay off the remaining loan balance of 151k and keep the 149k as profit and use it to buy a new house or put in the bank. This is one of the reasons home loans are considered good debt; because the home increases in value unlike cars, or clothes that we typically purchase. Now even in good debt, there is risk associated because the home's value can also drop.

Just like with any significant purchase, do your research. The point is you want to limit the amount of bad debt like car loans and credit cards. As we know, very rarely, and I mean almost never, is your car worth more after you've kept it for 15 years. Hence, focus on the good debt such as mortgages. I have seen clients use the profits from their first home to buy another home in cash and now they have no mortgage, setting them up well for their retirement years.

CHAPTER 7
UNDERSTANDING INTEREST RATES

I'm writing to you at a time during the Covid 19 pandemic. It seems ironic that I'm writing a book about finances during a period where we're dealing with the greatest health care crisis, which brought along with it the greatest financial crisis that we have ever witnessed. For many of us, this is the first time we have seen unemployment rate at 14.7% this is according to the bureau of labor statistics. It is also the first time we have seen millions of Americans sick or infected with a virus—and it's happening all around the globe. I say all this only to bring into focus the importance of planning and being able to stick to a long term plan because as this has proven, we cannot predict the future as much as we'd all wish we could. I'm thoroughly convinced, and call me biased because I am a financial adviser, that this proves the importance of seeking help from an expert to go over strategies and ways to keep your plan going in the event of the unthinkable happening.

One of the tools that has been used during this pandemic by the Federal Reserve is the lowering of interest rates; and part of the reason they've done that is to keep the economy afloat. Lowering interest rates makes borrowing money more attractive to big corporations, small businesses owners, and home buyers. It encourages companies to not lay off employees but instead, borrow money at a very low rate to fund projects and keep production going. This helps to stimulate the economy in a period where the consumer is not spending as much or in our case, has been quarantined and can't get out and spend.

What I have noticed about the lowering of interest rates is that, it is important to all of us. To the saver, lower interest rates means lower income since they have a large principle balance that they have been using to generate interests in order to supplement their social security and pension checks. Now, those rates have been slashed by the federal reserve when they cut the bank borrowing rate from 1.75 to .25 according to the washingtonpost.com. That is a decrease of roughly 85.5%. Imagine for a moment if you will; if you relied on the interests from your principal for income and in a flash, your interest rate was cut by 85%, that means your income has been cut by 85%. Many of us cannot withstand our income being cut by 85%. Now on the other hand, lower interest rates helps those of us who are in a good position and potentially looking to start a business or buy a home or even refinance the debt that we've accumulated over time into a lower rate. As a financial advisor, I've been forced to look at this from both sides of the coin because some of my clients are savers while others are young in the accumulation phase and looking to purchase their first home or consolidate debt that they have accumulated from a growing family. It's extremely important that we pay attention to the federal interest rates because they can help determine the financial decisions that we have to make in a world where there's a lot of noise around us. We still need to be able to make smart financial decisions because what has been proven is that, we will overcome, but will we be in position to take advantage of the victory.

Take for instance someone who may have been struggling with credit card debt. The debt hasn't taken them under yet because they still have their job and income and hopefully their health. But with the low interest rates, they can consider consolidating the credit card debt. You need to look at your situation and do what will be best for you, even if it is consolidating your debt and taking advantage of the low interest rates; which in turn can give you a lower monthly payment or could reduce the amount of interest you're going to pay back for borrowing that money. Consolidation during low interest rate periods is an important factor, because it can allow you to put money back in your pocket or even allow you to take those dollars and apply them to other areas such as retirement, vacation, college, or building your emergency savings up. How to consolidate debt or get the best interest rate are important financial decisions that you can only make if you are well informed. If you choose to remain ignorant of the economic changes that are happening around us, it'll be almost impossible for you to make smart financial decisions that will benefit you in the future.

One of the things that has remained relatively strong during this pandemic has been housing prices. Currently, the housing market is still at an all-time high. Home prices are higher than they've ever been. Understanding why rates are low and what the current economic environment looks like can help you understand when or if you should make a major purchase; like buying a home. Some of you might ask, how can a lower rate help me with buying a house? Lower interest rates give you the ability to pay less money back to the bank. This actually lets your dollar go further. Let me give you an example.

Let's takes someone who's paying a rent of $1500 a month, and want to buy a house. They want to stay in their budget of $1500 a month. If this person was to go out and look at a home during a period when interest rates are high, their buying power would decreased. But when interest rates are low, their buying power will increased. Let's put that into numbers. Presently, I can go out and get a 30-year fixed mortgage right around 3% if I wanted to buy a $350,000 house with a 30-year fixed mortgage. At a rate of 3%, my monthly payment would be roughly around $1476. Now let's just say rates increased just buy 1%. Even though it's not a whole lot of a change, a 1% increase lowers my purchasing power; so the same $350,000 house on a 30 year fixed mortgage at 4% will now cost me $1671 a month, which is outside my budget. This example shows you that an increase in interest rates can reduce your purchasing power; which means you can now no longer afford the home you were originally looking to buy since your limit was $1500 a month. I gave you this example to show you that interest rates can help you understand your purchasing power and help you make smarter financial decisions.

The reason I say making smarter financial decisions around interest rates can help shape your future is because a lower interest rate also means that you're going to be paying back less money to the institution you borrow from; which in turn means you can build equity in your home faster. This allows you to pay down the principal faster. Let's go back to our example of the $350,000 house being purchased with a 30-year fixed mortgage at 3% and the other at 4%. Now, let's assume we've owned the home for 10 years. How much have we paid down in those ten years? In the example of the 350k at 4%, at the end of 10 years, you would still owe $272,722. Now with the home for 350k at 3%, you would owe $262,815 after ten years. So, if your home is still valued at 350k and you bought at 4%, you would have $77,278 in positive equity in the home. On the other hand, if you bought the same home at 3%, you would have $81,185. This is a difference of $3,907. In many cases, the difference in the interest rates are generally not so close, but I used the 1% difference example to show you that even the smallest increase or decrease in interest rates can have an impact on your future decisions. Using that same example, let's assume that home's values, 10 years from now, are no longer at an all-time high. Instead, it is being valued at $325,000. Can you decide that your family has grown and it's time to sell this house and get something bigger? Well of course, you have to pay off the amount you owe, and wouldn't you want to owe less? I know the obvious answer is 'of course yes who doesn't want to owe less', but I only bring this up to put in perspective that choosing to purchase a home or make a financial decision without being aware of the current economic environment is in a sense, foolish, because it makes future decisions more difficult. Being informed can help you have a greater chance of success 10 or 20 years down the road all because you started with a smart and thought out foundation.

We have focused mainly on the advantages of low interest rates which helps those who are looking to purchase a home or consolidate debt, and how they can truly benefit from low rates and set themselves up for future success. Now, let's take a look at the other side of the coin. The savers of the world are those who have already bought their homes, paid their mortgage off years ago, and are retired; living on social security and possibly, a pension. So basically, they live on a fixed income which means their income doesn't change over time by very much. Therefore to help offset the rising cost of living, the savers supplements their fixed income through interest earned from savings that they have accumulated over time. They use the interest from the large principal balance to fill the gaps that social security and pension can't cover. As we said before, the lowering of interest rates for the saver is like a pay cut. Many of us know what it is like to take a pay cut, while our expenses remain the same. So the question we have is, if I'm a saver how do I supplement my income in a low interest rate environment? As a financial advisor one of the things I've noticed is that, as savers get older, they keep their investments mainly in bank products such as savings accounts & CDs. Now from a perspective of safety, I completely understand; this is because with bank products, you do not have to worry about the market value of their accounts changing day-to-day. But you can never be completely void of risk—and the risk banks are exposed to, is interest rate risk, which is what we are faced with today. One of the ways to avoid interest rate risk is to have a diverse group of products; bank accounts, investment accounts, and maybe an annuity. The main point I'm trying to make is that if you have a long term plan in place, it would have already addressed the potential impact of interest rate risk. However, in many cases, I see savers putting all their eggs in one basket to avoid risk, only to exposes themselves to risk anyway. Ultimately, my first favorite solution would be; before you begin the retirement phase of life, start with a long-term financial plan which would address the potential risk. It would look not just two years from now, but ten years or 20 years down the road and your plan would have taken the risk into account in your overall strategy.

Well, let's say you didn't have a chance to do that and your faced with the lower interest's environment. One way to look at it would be to first find out how much interest you need annually to fill the gap or supplement your fixed income. Once you know how much interest you need to make every year, you can then take the large balance and ladder those dollars from short term products to long term products. In a low interest rate environment, most places don't pay high fixed rates unless you are willing to hold those funds for a longer term. Let me give you an example of what that looks like. Let's say a saver has $200,000 that is kept in a bank account, and last year, they were earning 2% a year; which is a total of $4000 annually or $333.33 monthly. In 2019, many banks were paying rates of 2%, but now in year 2020, you can't get those rates at all from your bank. So from the example, I know I need to get to $4000 in interest annually to keep my income the same. But the question is, how do I get to that magic $4000 a year? Currently, the highest savings account according to bankrate.com, is paying 1.05% a year. And from annuity.org, the highest A rated company is paying 2.75%for a 5-year multiyear guaranteed annuity. This means the saver would have to put 150k in the 5-year guaranteed annuity and 50k in the savings account. The annuity will generate $4125 per year in interest and the savings account will generate $500 a year, giving the saver a total of $4625 a year. So by being able to understand interest rates in the current economic environment, the saver can put some of their dollars away for a longer term; giving them a higher return on their money while keeping some dollars in savings as an emergency fund. This example only further drives home my point of being educated and understanding the current economic environment so that you can make smart financial decisions no matter what is going on around you.

This example is for illustrative purposes only and the return is not indicative of any actual investment. Actual investment results may differ substantially.

CHAPTER 8
RISK VS REWARD

Most of the time, you see risk versus reward. But I think it's risk and reward since risk is not against reward. The two are married and they go hand-in-hand, therefore, it's risk and reward. When it comes to investing, there is an inherent risk; and the type of investment determines the type of risk. There are aggressive investments and there are also conservative investments; and there are some that fall in between the two. So before you even consider what you want to invest in, you must first consider how much risk you are willing to take. Let's think of what the bank offers, which is considered to be safe. The bank offers you CDs that are protected by FDIC insurance. This means that your principle, which is the money you invest, is never at risk and you can never get back less than what you put in. So a CD has no risk, but that's also why CDs pay very little interests. In this case, we see risk and reward married together, given that you have taken no risk and you've received very little reward. When you think of an individual stock, you are taking more risk since you're putting all your money into one company which has unlimited money making potential on the upside, but also has the potential to go to zero on the downside. It means that you can make a lot of money, you can make a little bit of money or lose all of your money. Not all stocks have the same amount of risk. for instance company A, may be a very large company with a proven track record of earnings. These types of companies may have less risk than say, your startup companies like Company B for example. Company B is a much smaller company without a proven track record of earnings, which means you still have the upside potential, but you could have a greater risk for loss because they are still in the growth phase. To break that down, think of it like this; there's a restaurant you've been to a dozen times say, Outback or Red Lobster. When you go there, you know the food's going to be good because they've been around for a long time and you even know the menu. But then a new restaurant you've never heard of opens up down the street. You will hesitate to go there since you don't know what they're known for or what's on their menu. In comparison, you have a greater risk of disappointment at the new restaurant than going to Outback or Red Lobster where you know what to expect. I know when I'm looking to have a good meal, I like to go places that I've already been to because I know what to expect. This way, I'm taking very little risk on being disappointed. But let's say one day you're feeling adventurous and you decide to try out the new restaurant and their food turns out to be delicious. You'll start thinking, man, this place is going to blow up once people find out about it! So just like in our example of Company B vs Company A ,A is the option that everyone knows very well hence, it may carry less risk. Company B, on the other hand, is the option you know less about but once you try it, you'll think it's wonderful, it has great upside potential but also great potential risk since everyone may enjoy it as much as you. This is a prime example of how two similar stocks can have different levels of risk.

You might be asking yourself, how do I keep my potential for upside but reduce my risk? Mutual funds may be an option which we discussed in the investing chapter. You can invest in Mutual funds that invest in a broad range of companies this way, you spread your risk out.

CHAPTER 9
INVESTING

When it comes to investing, it would be hard not to mention that Blacks make up about 13% of the US population, but only 3% of the nation's wealth. I'll give you just a minute to take that in. Yes, I said only 3% of the wealth in the US is owned by African Americans. The median household wealth for an African American is about $24,100 whereas the median household wealth for any non-African or non-Hispanic American is $188,200 according to Brookings.edu 2019 study. Likewise, when it comes to the investing world, African Americans only represent about 10% of the overall taxable investing population according to Finra.org. So, let's dig in a little bit about investing so we can change that narrative. In order to do this, we're going to have to start with the basics. So first, let's define the word 'stock'. Stock is used by business or corporation to raise capital by issuing shares of stock. Those shares represent a percentage of ownership of the business or corporation. Don't worry, I know what you're thinking—what the heck does that mean? Let me you give an example. Everyone has that uncle or cousin that always has a great new business they want you to lend them money for. Well in truth, this is not much different from a business or corporation issuing shares so they can raise money (also called capital) to fund the future growth of the business. One of the main differences between a corporation and your cousin who wants to borrow money is that, corporations issues documents on a regular basis showing how much profit they plan to bring in each quarter, and they go ahead to announce this information publicly. When you purchase a share of stock in any publicly traded company, you now become an owner of this particular company. You share in the profits of the company based on the number of shares of stock you own. By now, I bet you're wondering, how does a 'stock' make you money? So let me put this in terms you might understand better. Say you bought a pair of retro Jordan 11s (space jams) for $220 and you kept them for a year. They're in great condition and now you want to sell them. Those Jordan 11s now sell for $300, online. You would make a profit of $80 if you sold them. The value of the Jordan's appreciated over time, the same can happen with a stock. The price of the stock appreciates(rises) based on how well or how profitable the business or corporation is. Before you go through your closet looking for your old Jordans, let's take a look at an actual stock and how it performed over the last year. If I bought Company X last year in January 2019, it would have cost me $156 for 1 share. That means I paid $156 to be an owner of Company X, therefore, now I can hold on to that share until I'm ready to sell it. Let's say I held on to the share for one year. In January of 2020, Company X is selling for $316. If I choose to sell that share that I bought for $156 that is now worth

$316, I would make a profit of $160. This example is for illustrative purposes only and the return is not indicative of any actual investment. Actual investment results may differ substantially.

You don't have to be an expert in finance to know that you doubled your money. Who doesn't like that? I hope this makes some of you hesitate before you go out and buy your next pair of Jordans. Now I can't just tell you about the good parts when it comes to investing in stock. I also have to tell you the fact that you can buy a stock and your money could depreciate in value.. It can decrease in value or even go to zero—this is called risk. All investments have different levels of risk. We will cover risk more in depth in a later chapter. Before that, we are going to spend some time discussing stocks and a way to identify if it is worthy of your investment.

CHAPTER 10
STOCKS

What is a stock? Stock is equity ownership in a company. If I own one stock or share of a company, I'm considered an owner. As an owner, I'm entitled to receive or benefit from the growth of the company which is reflected in the stock price or share price. Hence, if I buy 100 shares of a company for 10 dollars per share, then my investment cost equals $1,000. If the price rises to 12 dollars per share, then my 100 shares of Nike are now worth $1,200. That means if I sold those shares at 12 dollars per share, I would get a profit of 200 dollars. Now if those shares went down to 9 dollars per share, then my 100 shares are only worth $900; and if I sold them at that price, then I would have lost 100 dollars.

When you look at buying individual stocks, one option may be to start with companies that have products you already use. Peter Lynch has been a top mutual fund manager for many years. He advises people to look for products that they normally buy, and then see who makes the product. He used this method because in most cases, you're not the only one who is buying that product. Your purchase is possibly one of the million purchases that turn into revenue. The revenue that's created from the millions of purchases ultimately can become profit for that company. This profit is one of the factors that drive a company's stock price. Once you have identified a company you're interested in, let the research begin. There are several ways, using today's technology, to help you identify if a stock is a promising investment. First, we must understand that a stock price reflects the potential future growth of the company. The price you see online contains the future potential earnings calculated into the price. This means the price you see is inflated; because it includes value that the company has not earned yet. So just using stock price alone to determine if you should buy a stock can prove harmful since none of us have a crystal ball to predict the future. We need to comprehend that a stock can be undervalued or overvalued. Undervalued is when a stock trades at a price that does not properly reflect its true growth potential. I call this "a discount" or "on sale". Overvalued is when a stock trades above its future growth potential, meaning the stock price is considered expensive. Identifying if a stock price is low or expensive is important. The old saying is, "Buy low and sell high." One of the most common ways to identify if a stock is cheap or expensive would be using the price-to-earnings ratio. This measures the company's current per-share price (stock price) to its per-share earnings. A company's P/E ratio can help you determine if the stock price is overvalued or undervalued. Let's use Company A in this example. Let's assume the current P/E ratio is 20. This means it is currently trading at 20 times its future earnings. A better way to show this; assume apple stock price was $200 per share and their earnings per share was $10, the price-to-earnings ratio would be 20. This means if I buy the stock for $200, I'm paying $20 for every dollar of earnings. Since the stock price of $200 includes the future earnings, if they fall short on earnings, the stock price will have to come down. Here is a different example. Take a pair of Yeezy boost, which cost $220 at the time of writing this. But the cost of producing a pair of Yeezy Boost is $35. That means we pay 6 times what it cost to produce the shoes. In my culture, we call that a serious upcharge. The price of $220 is the price we as consumers are willing to pay for the shoes. Consumers are willing to pay 6 times what it costs to produce a single pair of Yeezy Boost. And considering they have sold out year after year, the demand for the shoes has justified the price. If the demand for Yeezy Boost went down, then in order to encourage consumers to buy them again, the price would be lowered. The same happens to stocks; when the demand for the stock decreases, the price is lowered essentially. When you are looking at a stocks' price, knowing if the stock is overvalued or undervalued can help reduce your risk if the company has poor performance and does not produce the earnings anticipated. It can also help you to know if the stock is discounted and whether it's a good time to buy. When a stock has a low P/E ratio, it can mean it is undervalued. The stock could potentially be worth more than what the price reveals. This is possible when the company has better than anticipated the growth. When that happens, the price has to increase to reflect the stock's true value. It is best to compare the P/E ratio to the company's competitor's and use analyst reports as a guide in determining if the P/E ratio is high or low.

As in the example with Company A, the P/E ratio was 20, but the previous year it was 23.20. So for, a 20 P/E ratio might indicate undervalue. I bring this up because one of the key things to remember is that you have to research, especially if you want to buy individual stocks. Individual stocks do produce the most growth potential, but also carry the most risk. You work hard for your money so put in a couple of hours a week and research your stocks before you make a purchase; and even after you purchase the stock, continue to research your investment.

CHAPTER 11
BONDS

When you are being the successful businessperson that you are, people always come to you asking to borrow money. You normally say no but this time you say yes, though it comes with a condition. You want a repayment by a certain date, you want the interest paid every 6 months, and you get to set the interest rate. Now many people I know would look at me cross eyed if I was to have such requirements. This is exactly what a company or the US government does when they want to borrow money and don't want to take out a loan from a bank—they issue a debt also known as bonds. A bond is an agreement of repayment made by the US government, corporations or municipalities. These bonds are used to fund city transportation, build factories, and even football stadiums. The way a bond works is like this; a company says let us borrow $1,000 for 10 years. And for every year we hold your $1000, we will give you a 3% interest which equals 30 dollars; and at the end of those 10 years, will give you your $1000 back. In total, you made $300 on your $1,000 because they paid you a total of $300 in interest. Bonds are considered to be conservative investments. Why would a company do this, especially the ones that have cash? Let's say a company wants to build a new factory, and these factories cost hundreds of millions of dollars. Just like you and I don't like spending all our savings, companies don't either; and it is generally not recommended because in the event of an emergency, the well would be dry. What they might do instead is pay cash for part of the project and finance the rest with debt or a bond offering. When a company offers a bond, they set the term or maturity date say, 5 or 20 years from now. They also say how much interest they are willing to pay every year until the bond matures. Once these bonds are issued, the company is now obligated to pay interest semi-annually and pay the purchaser back their principal at maturity. The good news is that, bonds, once owned are not as volatile as the stock market. The bond is a fixed instrument. As said before, the company that offers the bond must pay the interest they originally said in the initial creation of the bond. Bonds work to help support a portfolio by minimizing the volatility, and also can be used as a stream of income since most bonds pay out semi-annually.

The return and principal value of bonds fluctuate with changes in market conditions. If bonds are not held to maturity, they may be worth more or less than their original value.

CHAPTER 12
LIFE INSURANCE

Now I know at least one of you has been to a funeral or had a loved one pass away and before the funeral started; they set up a GoFundMe account, or they passed around a hat, or they called the Uncle who has money to help pay for the funeral. So not only does the bereaved family have to deal with the loss, they also have to deal with the bill as well. Though the death could not have been prevented, the bill could have been taken care of had a life insurance policy been put in place prior to their death. Too many times I have heard or been a part of someone passing that did not have life insurance. Let's first understand the purpose of a life insurance. Life insurance is for the benefit of the living; it is there to protect your physical assets and the living assets, meaning your family. With a proper life insurance policy in place, the gap of the loss of income can be filled, the house can be paid off, and the kids can be sent to college. As a parent myself, it is my duty to protect my family, which is fairly easy since I'm living and my income helps to provide for my family's needs. But if I were to die today, my life insurance policy would help cover those same needs. Life insurance is the cheapest when you buy it while you're young and healthy. If you wait until you get older, possible health issues could arise and you can potentially become uninsurable; and not to mention, it cost more when you're older. There are two main types of life insurance; one is called permanent insurance or whole life and the other is called term life insurance. We will discuss each one of these separately so you can get a good understanding of how they work, how they're different, and how they're similar. But I can say this; having one or the other is better than nothing. As an adviser, many times I hear "Well, I have life insurance on my job." Life insurance through your work, in most cases, is not portable. Meaning if you leave your job, you can't take it with you. If for any reason you happen to have a health issue that arises and you can't continue to work and you have to leave that job, then you no longer have a life insurance policy and you could potentially be uninsurable. That is why it's very important that you have a policy that is outside of your workplace that's already in place. This way, in the event that something happens to you, health wise, you already have a policy that's ready to work for you in the untimely event of your death. I know this is not a fun subject for anyone to talk about, but it is necessary we do. If we don't talk about it, how can we ever plan and protect the family that we so love? Life insurance is also a very good way to pass on wealth; it has tax benefits for those who receive it. The main benefit is that the life insurance received by the beneficiary is not taxed. Yes, that's right, no taxes. So your loved ones can receive this money tax free. A good example would be to say a 45-year-old man who has two children (16 and 13) and a wife that he supports with his income unfortunately gets into a car accident and passes away. Now his youngest child will not be 18 for another 5 years. And when he passed away, he left behind a mortgage and future college expenses, and not to mention, his wife now has to deal with the loss of his income. If he had no life insurance, he left a great burden behind for his family. Now let's assume he had a $500,000 insurance policy. With these funds, his wife would be able to pay off the mortgage, and fund a college savings account for the kids. She would also be able to replace his income until she can start working. You don't have to be a rocket scientist to know that the second scenario with the life insurance policy in place is a much better way to take care of your family. Before you run out and buy a policy, a wise thing to do would be to estimate how much life insurance you really need. And to do that, a lot of the life insurance calculators take into account the loss of income, how much you owe on the home, how old your kids are and if you want to leave money behind for your kids for college or other goals you want to take care of for your kids. This needs to be done so that you only pay for the amount of insurance that will help you accomplish those goals and protect your family, though there is such a thing as too much insurance. After you run your life insurance estimate, the next thing you want to do is discuss the type of insurance you want to have, and that goes back to our discussion of the types of insurance (term or whole life insurance). In the next two chapters, we will discuss these two types of insurance and this will help you make a good financial decision when you go to purchase a policy. Now that you know the importance of life insurance, let's get into how it works. When you buy an insurance policy, the amount you insured is called the death benefit; this is what is paid out to your beneficiaries. The amount you pay every month for the policy to stay active is called your premium. No matter the type of insurance you buy, there will be a death benefit and a premium—this is part of the contract. The life insurance company is entering into a promise or contract with you to pay your beneficiaries the death benefit as long as your contract is active and paid up. This is very similar to how car insurance works, except this time, the contract is tied to your life.

The cost and availability of life insurance depend on factors such as age, health, and the type and amount of insurance purchased. Before implementing a strategy involving life insurance, it would be prudent to make sure that you are insurable by having the policy approved. As with most financial decisions, there are expenses associated with the purchase of life insurance. Policies commonly have mortality and expense charges. In addition, if a policy is surrendered prematurely, there may be surrender charges and income tax implications.

CHAPTER 13
TERM LIFE INSURANCE

Term life insurance is just what it sounds like. It is a life insurance policy that covers a set term or a period of time. Typically, Term insurance is sold in 10, 20, or 30-year blocks. It is mostly used when a family is growing, and they have young kids or a mortgage and very little monetary assets. Term can be used to protect your young growing family. Usually, families with young children have more debt because catering for kids is expensive—yep, I said it. Term is typically cheaper than whole life insurance since it is only insuring you for a set period of time; like the next 20 years of your life, then it ends. The insurance company behind the scenes has people who work for them called actuaries. These people help to determine the risk associated with a person potentially dying during the chosen period of time. Once that period of time ends, so does the policy. Many companies will offer you a chance to renew the policy after the term, but the rates are renegotiated and, in most cases, it is much higher than you were paying originally. This happens because you're older now and the risk of insuring you has changed. The advantages to term life insurance is that you can get a lot of insurance coverage for a fairly reasonable price. The disadvantage is that the Term ends after a set period of time, which by then, you'll be 10, 20 or 30 years older and will still need a policy to cover your family. You won't need as much coverage as you did when your kids were young or when you still owed money on the house, but you still need a policy to at least cover your funeral cost (which can be 10k or more), or serve as a source of income for your surviving spouse.

CHAPTER 14
WHOLE LIFE INSURANCE

Whole life insurance also means just that; it covers your whole life, unlike Term which is a set number of years. Whole life has some features that differ from Term life. Firstly, it does not end after a set number of years as long as the premiums are paid up. Secondly, whole life can build up a cash value balance. This can be done due to your monthly premiums. Part of your premium pays for the companies cost to insure you and the remaining amount goes to a cash value account. Let me break it down. If you pay $100 every Month, $75 goes to pay for the cost to insure you and $25 goes to your cash value balance. And this is done over a period of 12 Months for the next 10 years. So as you can imagine, the $25 that you're paying every month to your cash value after 10 years will have built up to quite a bit, not to mention, the insurance company is paying you interests on the cash value which is compounding. The cash value that's being built up is money you can borrow or even withdraw.

Whole life can be significantly higher per month than term—and NO, that does not mean Whole life is bad. The cost difference is because the insurance company is no longer just looking at your life for a set number of years like with term. But instead, they are basing the cost of insurance on your entire life, which I think we all can agree that doing this involves more risk for the insurance company. Like in the $100 monthly premium example made earlier, your money would buy more insurance coverage with a Term policy, but at some point, the policy would end. Whole life can be more expensive, but it never goes away; meaning you will never have to buy another insurance later down the road. The key thing you want to make sure you focus on, is having enough coverage to protect your family. Generally, a growing family with dependents (that if one of the income earners died unexpectedly could leave behind a financial burden) would use Term insurance during the high-risk period so they can get a larger death benefit. They would also have a smaller whole life policy for when that term ends to cover funeral expenses. It's important you work with a life insurance agent or a financial advisor to calculate your insurance needs. You may decide to use both Term and Whole life in your protection strategy. I have given you the basics on whole life insurance but, truthfully a separate book can be written on insurance alone. The takeaway I want you to have is that, Life insurance can be affordable and is necessary for the protection of your family. You don't want to leave a burden for your spouse or your children. The loss of a loved one is devastating enough, don't make the living suffer further by making them give up on dreams and aspirations because they can no longer afford to.

CHAPTER 15
RETIREMENT PLANNING

So often, when I am working with clients that are just starting out on their retirement journey or have very little experience saving for retirement, but have a lot of experience working the question; the question I often ask is, "Are you contributing to your 401K, and does your company offer a match?" Often, the answer is "no" and I always ask why—it's free money. I know when I say the term "free money", some of you may say it's not free since you have to work for it. Yes, that's true. But if you're going to work in and your company's going to match what you contribute to your own retirement, why not take advantage of it? I know when I say the term free money some of you may say it's not free I have to work for and yes that's true but if you're going to work in your company's going to match what you contribute to your own retirement why not take advantage of it.

What is a match? A match is when your employer agrees to put money in your 401K up to a certain dollar amount or percentage, based on your contributions. Let me show you how this works. Let's say you make $50,000 a year and you put in 6% of your salary which is $3,000, annually. Because you make this contribution to your retirement, your employer will match up to 6%. So that means if you put in 6%, they will match it with 6%, which is a total of 12% ($6,000) being contributed to your retirement or 401k. The 6% ($3,000) the employer put in is the "free money". This type of match would be considered a full match because the employer matches dollar for dollar up to a certain percentage. Some employer plans only offer a partial match. In this type of match, your employer will require you to contribute a certain percentage in order for them to give a partial match. To explain this more clearly, let's use the example above of an annual salary of $50,000. If you contribute 6%, your company will match 3% of your contribution, which equals 50% of your contribution. This means your total contribution to your following 401K is 9%. In order to receive the 3%, you must put in at least 6%. Every employer plan is different, so you must check with your human resources department in order to find out what your company does offer for a match. The match can be a huge benefit and boost to your retirement. You will add to your overall balance of your 401K, which allows it to grow faster. Many companies use the matching as a benefit to attract talent to the company. You should consider the match as a way to fast track yourself to retirement. It's basically your company giving you free money toward your future retirement. Why wouldn't you take it?

Let's see how a 'retirement plan without a match' looks, and compare it with the previous example. Just like in the first example, we will assume you make $50,000 a year. You're 35 years old and plan to retire at age 67. You contribute 6% of your income to your retirement plan, but your company doesn't offer a matching plan. If you earned at least 5% return on your investments in your 401k, you would have saved $225,896.49—not bad. Now let's look at the same example, but let's assume the company now matches you with 6%. Your 401k savings would be $451,792.98—this is a much better-looking number. This shows you how the "free money" or the company match can boost your retirement and help you reach your goals faster.

This example is for illustrative purposes only and the return is not indicative of any actual investment. Actual investment results may differ substantially.

The next major question I usually receive about matching contributions is, "Do I get to keep it?" The answer is it depends. The contributions you put into the 401k are always yours to take with you to another job. The free money or the company's contributions can be immediately vested, meaning they are all yours. In other cases, the company can establish a vesting schedule which basically means you have to meet a certain number of years of service before the company's contributions can be 100% yours. The immediate vesting is the best type of vesting schedule, but either way, the company is offering you free money—you should be involved. To many times, I have seen clients not have enough to live the retirement lifestyle they want. This could be as a result of them starting too late or not taking advantage of the match program because it wasn't something they fully understood. Matching programs are very common today. They are essential to an employee's retirement, especially in a world were pension plans are rare, and we will most likely in the near future have to generate most of our income from our 401ks. The African American culture statistically is less likely to participate in the 401k plan or get the match because of the perceived risk associated with the 401k investments. This lack of participation only further widens the wealth gap between African Americans and White Americans. Although retirement savings in America is already low, African Americans and Hispanics save the least in 401k plans. The benefits offered through the 401k plan are vital, especially if the employer offers a matching contribution plan. Working with the company's financial advisor or one you already know can really help when it comes to choosing your contribution amount and the investments inside your 401k plan. The investments can be designed to fit your comfort level. If we want to increase our wealth and leave a legacy, then retirement savings using the 401k and employer matching programs, is the key place to start.

Distributions from traditional IRA's and employer sponsored retirement plans are taxed as ordinary income and, if taken prior to reaching age 59 ½, may be subject to an additional 10% IRS tax penalty.

CHAPTER 16
TYPES OF RETIREMENT PLANS

According to the small business administration, 33% of Americans work for a small business. 70% of all US businesses are owned by non-minorities and 9.5% are owned by African Americans. The number of small businesses owned by minorities, as well as the number of non-minority owners striking it out, is increasing rapidly. Whether you work for a small business or you own one, you need an exit strategy. The recent move from corporate jobs to business ownership has made planning for retirement your responsibility. There are very few—if any—retirement plans left that allow you to take a hands-off approach. The lack of retirement plans offered by small business owners who usually employ majority-minority workers, only widens the wealth gap. For most of us, our greatest source of wealth outside of our home value is our retirement funds. This is why you must know and understand the retirement options that are available to you. Many of us say we want to retire one day. If we don't take actionable steps and start planning, then I assure you; it won't happen. Working with a financial advisor can help you find out which plan is best for you but first, you need to understand the basics of your options.

If you are self-employed or own a business, you have a few different options to consider.

1. Traditional IRA- A Traditional Individual Retirement account allows you to put money away for your retirement. The contributions can be deducted from your income tax. This type of retirement plan allows you to benefit now by decreasing your reportable income by the amount of your contribution. The money also grows tax-deferred. Which means you will pay taxes on any distribution. There are contribution limits of $6,000 a year if you are under age 50, and $7,000 a year if you're 50 years or older. If you take money out of the IRA before you turn 59 ½ years old, you pay a 10% penalty tax. After age 59 ½, you only have to pay taxes on the money you take out that year. This type of retirement account works well for someone looking to reduce their income tax burden, while saving for their future.

2. Roth IRA - this type of retirement account is after-tax; this means you do not get to deduct the contributions from your income. The benefit here is seen once you retire since your withdrawals will be tax-free. There are also contribution limits of $6,000 a year if you are 50 years or below, and $7,000 a year if you are 50 years or older. Roth IRAs can work well for someone who expects to have a high income during

retirement since these funds can be withdrawn after 59 ½, and are tax-free.

3. Simple IRA- this works very much like the Traditional IRA as far as the pretax benefits goes. But with the Simple IRA, it benefits both the employer and employee because it allows a matching contribution at dollar for dollar up to 3% from the employer to the employee. Simple IRA does require employer contributions for employees who opt in the plan. The business can deduct those contributions. The employee can also make pre-tax contributions which would be deducted from the employee's taxable income. Employees can contribute a maximum of $13,500 annually in 2021. If you are 50 years or older, you may make an additional catch-up contribution of $3,000, bringing your annual maximum to a total of $16,500.

The business has to have 100 or fewer employees.

4. SEP (Simplified Employee Pension) IRA- this account works like the Traditional IRA, but has a much higher contribution limit. Contributions made by employers cannot exceed the lesser of: 25% of an employee's compensation, or $58,000 in 2021. These contributions are tax deductible. This plan also allows the employer discretion on contributions, based on the business profits.

These four plans are simple and easy to setup, have low expenses, and work best for smaller companies.

5. 401k plan- this is a company sponsored retirement plan. Employees make pre-tax contributions and the employer can make matching contributions to the account. The maximum amount that an employee or

employer can contribute to a 401(k) plan. As of 2020 and in 2021, the basic limits on employee contributions are $19,500 per year for workers under age 50, and $26,000 for those who are 50 years and above (including the $6,500 catch-up contribution). This plan can have administrative fees and other cost associated with it. Generally, larger businesses benefit from this type of plan.

This is a brief overview of some of the retirement plan options you have as a business owner. These plans can provide a retirement future for you and your employees. It's best to work with a financial advisor to help figure out which plan will benefit you most.

CHAPTER 17
BUILD A TEAM

We all need a team. I recall an episode of 'Martin', a 90s TV show that starred Martin Lawrence. In this episode, he got a speeding ticket and he did not want to pay. He decided to take it to court and challenge the ticket in the hopes that the officer who issued the ticket would not show up and he would win by default. Of course, he lost because the officer showed up. Martin, who was not a lawyer did a terrible job of trying to represent himself in the courtroom. Let me ask you, do you find yourself trying to do things to save a buck when you know this requires a trained professional? African Americans have a legacy of distrust. Very often, we are hesitant to use an expert; whether it's a doctor, an accountant, to name a couple. Why is this? Some might say it's just the way we were brought up and others might say it's about price. I think it's a combination of both. Often times, if our parents lived on check to check, then you never heard dad say, "honey remind me to call the accountant."

Most of the time, our parents did the taxes on their own. For many different reasons, our culture has avoided and grown distrust with professionals, which I think in a lot of instances, has created a disadvantage. Can you really build wealth, or compete with the top businesses by only relying on the information you already possess? If you're going to start your own business, invest in the stock market, or even buy a house, you need the right team. Like in basketball, Lebron didn't win a championship all by himself. He needed a team to help carry the load. Sometimes, we get upset when people tell us to hire an accountant or go see a lawyer, because in our heads, we're thinking "I'm just as smart as them. Why do I need to pay someone?" You might be just as smart as the lawyer or accountant, but they are experts in their field. Instead, we go to YouTube to learn the rules that the experts already know. When competing in the business world or trying to find the right investment, there is a reason why some people consistently succeed. Those who usually see consistent success have realized that their time is better invested in the things they do best. 65% of small businesses fail in the first 10 years according to Investopedia.com.

This can mostly be attributed to four key reasons.

1. Financial difficulties: a lot of business owners are good at making the product, but are unclear on how much revenue they need to generate on a monthly or annual basis to maintain staff or inventory. This leads to financial hardship and eventually, the doors close.

2. Poor marketing: as a business owner, you're

focused on your clients who visit your establishment daily. But who is focused on growing your brand? Do you have time to learn all the ins and outs of Facebook marketing or figure out what works best on Instagram? You can rely on word of mouth, but that can only take your business so far.

3. Bad Management: not every owner is cut out to manage people. If your business requires staff, then they must be managed properly and effectively to maintain a level of success. Many owners have the skills needed to manage, but lack the time necessary to do so because their business is growing and pulling them in many different directions.

4. No Business plan: many businesses start up without a clear plan other than to provide goods and service to generate revenue. You need a plan that grows with the business and adapts to the ever-changing environment and competition. The Covid 19 pandemic has taught all of us that things can change in a flash. Does your business plan incorporate this kind of disruption? We all saw some restaurants quickly switch over to online ordering and delivery because they had already implemented these services. At the same time, we saw some businesses fail to make these adjustments, closing their doors at the end.

These are just the four main reasons, according to the Small business administration. But I think the list can be even longer. The takeaway is that, in life or in business, you need a team. Hire an accountant to handle the finances, track revenue and do the taxes. Hire an office manager to manage day to day operations. Use a marketing company to develop a strategy that gets your company in front of many people as possible. Work with a business consultant to develop a business plan so you can avoid pitfalls. Experts have the experience needed to guide you so you can build your company, and focus on the part of the business that brings you the most joy as well.

There is power in partnership. Yet far too often, this is overlooked. As a kid, I enjoyed the old national geographic shows—I would watch them for hours. I recall an episode in which they covered the wolf. I watched as the lone wolf survived for a little while; catching small prey and having some success. But he was unable to take down any big prey since by himself, he was easy to fight off. Meanwhile, the pack of wolves working together to track large caribou had repeated success, feeding themselves and their young pups. Many times, we act like the lone wolf; trying to make it in this harsh environment on our own. We will have some success, but it's only just enough to sustain us; it's not enough to give us surplus so we can feed ourselves and those around us. The success of the wolf pack proves that when you work with the right partners, you can accomplish bigger goals. The right partner can help you get a surplus; and when the tough times come, you can live off your surplus. This applies to our lives in so many ways. But from a financial perspective, it means; are you trying to do your own taxes? Are you trying create your debt pay-off strategy? Are you picking your own investments? Are you trying to manage your business and your staff alone? How good could you be if you partnered with someone you trust, and who allows you to focus on what you're good at? How much time could you save if you partnered with someone who was an expert in the area you're weak in? When you want to achieve great success, you need a team of partners because as you grow in wealth or in business, the issues you face become more complicated—and one critical mistake can tear down all you have built. When you think of partners for your team, it might be your local banker, your lawyer, your accountant, your financial advisor or a trusted mentor. It's best to establish these relationships early; even before you need them so you can develop trust. If you wait till a problem arises, you'll put yourself in a situation of need. Surround yourself with people who can help you and not drain you. You need to establish strategic partnerships to help you carry the financial responsibility. You don't have to be the lone wolf.

www.ingramcontent.com/pod-product-compliance
Lightning Source LLC
Chambersburg PA
CBHW020456220526
45464CB00002B/1005